THE

FEED YOUR MIND

THERAPY

FEED YOUR SOUL

OF

SHARE YOUR KNOWLEDGE

COOKING

THIS IS A THREE IN ONE BOOK:
MOTIVATIONAL, INSPIRATIONAL QUOTES
AND DELICIOUS RECIPES

Giovanni L Malacrino
Stephen Truelove

With thanks to

Martyn Ward for his honest and constructive advice,
without emotion.

Massimiliano Vian for his input on recipe ingredients and intolerances.

Laura Benito for the photography and video work.

Amanda Wightman for inspiring the well-being mini zoo for
children with disabilities.

Luca Malacrino for voice over (Audio Book).

Holly Weeks for her proofreading.

Adam Clarke for his cartoon illustration.

Jay Bevan for his ongoing assistance.

THE

FEED YOUR MIND

THERAPY

FEED YOUR SOUL

OF

SHARE YOUR KNOWLEDGE

COOKING

THIS IS A THREE IN ONE BOOK:
MOTIVATIONAL, INSPIRATIONAL QUOTES
AND DELICIOUS RECIPES

Giovanni L Malacrino
Stephen Truelove

Published by GMPF Limited

Published in 2019 by GMPF Limited. Company No. 10691806.

Copyright © Giovanni L Malacrino and Stephen Truelove 2019.

Giovanni L Malacrino and Stephen Truelove have asserted their right to be identified as the
authors of this work in accordance with the Copyright,
Designs and Patents Act 1988.

Printed in the UK by Inka Colour Print
Unit 17 – 20, Wernddu Court, Caerphilly CF83 3SG

Designed by: dianaedwardsdesign.co.uk

ISBN: 978-1-9162890-1-7

Contents

Giovanni L Malacrino

By the time I was twenty-one years old, I had travelled the world and met thousands of influential people, socialised and got paid for it.

In my late teenage years, I was working on luxury cruise liners. I was constantly on the move. By eighteen, I had bought my first house, which I paid off within four years. By twenty-two, I had opened my first restaurant in New Jersey U.S.A., with my great friend Ron Bird. I went on to open many more restaurants and nightclubs, as well as buying properties. At such a young age, I was unstoppable.

But in the midst of all my success, there was a shift in my emotional state.

I worried about losing my business, money, house, and health - 'how would I look after my child?' was my fear. I went on a downward spiral. I became depressed. I thought about all my years of being a successful, popular character and couldn't understand why I felt this way. Depression hit me so hard I spent three full days in bed, not wanting to move. Bound by negative thoughts, frustration, and confusion, I encountered my first motivational, life-changing book. It was called 'Personal Power' by Anthony Robbins. I realised my depression came from the best gift, which was my first child being born. I focussed on my child which motivated me to rise above it. I began to think "I can" rather than "I can't".

My positive change made me want to learn about my sub conscious. After years of overcoming my own personal challenges, running numerous businesses and by this time having two amazing children, I felt it was time to share what I have learnt so far. This book stems from my exciting journey through life and I hope it inspires you to achieve your dreams and get into that kitchen.

Stephen Truelove

A proud son of the South Wales Valleys, I have over eighteen years' experience helping people to be the best version of themselves, author of A Journey of Discovery and Self-Learning and developer of the Love Life Love You process, Breaking Limitations.

At seventeen I was married and a father, working with my Dad in electrical contracting at Port Talbot. Later I worked at GE Aviation Nantgarw, together with my brother Mark until his untimely death in a motorcycle accident aged just 39.

For seventeen years I worked my socks off providing for my family. Then it all fell apart. My marriage collapsed and I landed back at Mam and Dad's with three kids and a saxophone, feeling very sorry for myself. Somehow I managed to keep my job, but I was running on empty and in need of a bigger overhaul than any of the aircraft engines I was working on.

Fascinated by the power of the mind, I studied hypnotherapy, Reiki, Cognitive Behavioural Therapy and other techniques and learned a lot about myself. People saw the difference in me and wanted me to help them too. I also joined a band, Sounds Familiar, with whom I still play sax to this day.

The heart of my success as a therapist is removing limitations, releasing the inner brake that stops us being the best we can.
We know we can do the new job, yet something holds us back. We all want to go to the ball, but we make Cinderellas of ourselves without an ugly sister in sight. A little voice whispers: you're not good enough, not clever enough, not good looking enough, you're a girl, you're a boy – it won't work, don't even try. We can reprogram that voice.

Whether you want to lose a bit of weight or feel less anxious, or whether you need to pick yourself up from rock bottom as I did, we can help you take that step.

Giovanni and Stephen's initial introduction arose from the gut feeling of a couple of their mutual colleagues, Rob and Warren. The pair suggested Giovanni meet with Stephen, due to Giovanni's ongoing coaching and development with Anthony Robbins, Paul McKenna, Dr Richard Bandler and many other major life coaches. Giovanni attended Stephen's practice armed with pen, paper, and Dictaphone, prepared to assist Stephen in promoting himself.

After asking Stephen what was so different about his way of helping people, Giovanni eventually, and reluctantly, followed up on Stephen's suggestion to attend a session.

The session included Emotional Freedom Technique tapping and hypnotherapy amongst other unique techniques. At the time, Giovanni had just sold his nightclub chain and was going through major changes in his life.

"Quite often, as a life coach, we will throw our energy at helping other people, not realising we have a ton of stuff we haven't dealt with"

Giovanni L Malacrino

For the next few months following the pair's session, Giovanni's life began improving in areas he didn't realise he had challenges in.
He became the person he was before owning a chain of businesses.
The restaurateur and life coach was making more money, sleeping soundly and felt happier.

The creation of Giovanni's mini zoo for children with learning difficulties derived from Stephen's help. Giovanni went from running nightclubs to taking care of rabbits, chickens, ducks, pigs and lots more animals.

Giovanni's desire to write a book has always been hindered by his ADHD. The condition means he always has twenty projects going on, which take longer to complete than he would like. With the duo's combined experiences in therapy, and Stephen's ability to bring Giovanni back to the present, the pair set out to write this book. The idea behind the book is to combine two forms of therapy with a load of delicious food.

The idea came to Giovanni during the filming of his cooking show. He noticed his mind wandering off to different places, some positive, some not. He spoke to Stephen about his realisation. Stephen agreed that cooking in a bad mood creates unfulfilling food, adding one extra layer of stress on to an already dampened mental state. The pair made it their mission to figure out how you can bring your mind away from those negative places, to somewhere positive. This book holds the key to making that switch.

Stephen Truelove is a truly inspirational life coach and therapist; his never ending desire to support individuals tackle the numerous challenges that life throws at them, however common or unusual, really sets him apart in his field. I have worked with Stephen both professionally and personally, and wouldn't hesitate to recommend him wholeheartedly.

Greg Fisher, NFN Regional Employment Broker for Wales

Stephen Truelove is a very experienced and talented therapist. If this book served to help people in the way that Stephen does in other therapy settings, it is a highly recommendable read.

Dr Daniel Nightingale, PhD; RN; ADHP; Fellow of the Royal Society of Medicine Clinical Dementia Specialist General Psychotherapist

Wow. Steve was able to support me on a real intuitive level whilst using his vast skills and knowledge. Taking me through a journey of self discovery throughout the session. His ability to work through what I was going through helped shift things for me and I can't thank him enough for his kindness, professionalism and nature in his work.

Owen Morgan, World Health Heroes Founder

I have worked very closely with Steve over the years and have witnessed some life changing events that have been brought about through his vast experience knowledge and selfless efforts to help people to re-engage with the world and themselves, allowing the tides to turn in their lives and bring about positivity, well-being, happiness, wealth and love, but to mention a few, looking forward to reading the book as we can all benefit from the extra mile.

Rob Turner, Commercial Director

From the moment I met Stephen, I knew he had something special. A passionate and dedicated man who truly wants to make a difference in the world. He is not only exceptionally intuitive but a true master of his chosen field.

Jason Firmager, MD Holistic Therapist Magazine

Quietly confident and not given to blowing his own trumpet (though he's an enthusiastic saxophone player), Steve wears his qualifications and experience lightly. He never lets you feel that he knows it all and you don't, that he's OK and you're not, but shares what he has learnt to help you move forward. A straightforward bloke who gets results, Steve tells it how it is, without bullshit or psycho-babble, but with compassion, patience and endless good humour.

Vanessa Clarke, Editor

Giovanni is very proud of his Welsh/Italian heritage, an entrepreneur who has established a number of very successful businesses who in common with all entrepreneurs some of his ventures have had more success than others, however he has always bounced from challenges such as the redevelopment of the St David's centre that reduced footfall to zero outside two of his main restaurants and has fought off major competition from UK chain operators due to the integrity and quality of his food business. Great hospitality businesses are built on generosity and the owner building a culture of loyalty with the team, empowering and enabling them and creating an atmosphere of fun that customers enjoy and return to again and again .

Gio over the years has put a lot back into the city of Cardiff with Mill Lane and his support of charities, he brought Anthony Robbins to the city and the numerous young people that he has selflessly mentored sharing his wisdom and indeed his humility so they can learn from his life and business experience and recognise that resilience is essential in overcoming challenges and recognise that challenge is actually key to a rewarding life.

Ciaran Fahey, CEO Ritz Hotel

I've known Giovanni both as a friend and businessman for many years. He brought to Cardiff amazing Italian food and a tremendous passion to help others. He is a pioneer for Wales and goes on inspiring many, many people. I am sure this book will help change lives for the better...

Joe Calzaghe, The longest-reigning super-middleweight world champion in boxing history to date

---

There won't be many people in Cardiff who aren't aware of Giovanni. His infectious spirit has touched many across the city, and his warm and welcoming personality is one I'd like to think is analogous with the city itself.

Of course, Gio is more than just a personality. He's also made a huge personal contribution to our city, paving the way for our Café Quarter at Mill Lane, and introducing al-fresco dining not just to Cardiff, but also the nation. It's fair to say that his vision and determination has left a lasting impression and continues to do so. Put simply, without Giovanni Cardiff would be a less fun place to be.

My personal experience of working with Gio is hugely positive. He's very much a team player who understands that collaboration is not always the enemy of competition. He's also a leader, someone who the community can gather around to make a change. As a man who I know is passionate about Cardiff he is also a great advocate and ambassador, and undoubtedly an asset for our great city.

It is fitting that Gio's first book brings together two of his passions – food and well-being - two areas where he has made a big impact on in Cardiff. Through his words in this book he can now spread that passion further afield."

Jonathan Day, Economic Policy Manager / Rheolwr Polisi Economaidd - Economic Development / Datblygu Economaidd

Giovanni gives real meaning to the word gusto! It shows in his spirit, his company, his food, and his commitment to human well-being. It certainly shows in this book and I recommend his Therapy – for life as well as for cooking.

The Right Honourable, The Lord Kinnock PC. And Happy customer

---

Giovanni, or as I like to call him 'Mr Cardiff', is someone worth listening to. He sees problems as opportunities and then does something about it. He established Cardiff's Cafe Quarter by taking action and responsibility when others wouldn't. He learned to enrol others in his objectives and has always given something back.

His charity work is a big part of who he is which is why this book is worth using as he wants to make a difference. What can be more sociable than cooking and sharing thoughts? The world needs more of this.

Martyn Ward, Author and Businessman

I have known Giovanni for over thirty years and he is one of the most driven and charismatic characters I have ever met. He and I have become close friends.

Gio, as we call him, can reflect on the major influence he has been on shaping Cardiff's restaurants and night time economy. It was his idea to create the Cafe Quarter in Mill Lane which is now so well established as the go-to place to eat, drink and have fun and it has also become one of the most talked about experience for those visiting our City for the first time.

Gio's enthusiasm is infectious and he is passionate about Cardiff and his brand will be associated with our Capital City for ever, and I am proud to be his friend.

Nigel Roberts, Chairman of the Cardiff Business Council and serial entrepreneur

Giovanni Malacrino
with Luciano Pavarotti

Giovanni with legendary actor
Simon Callow CBE, star of Shakespeare
in love and Ace Ventura

Giovanni with TV Chef Steven Terry,
and David Pickering, WRU Chairman
of the board and former player

Giovanni & Sir Tom Jones
on one of his many visits

Giovanni with
Kara Tointon

Giovanni with Ed Sheeran
enjoying a take away

Giovanni & Sam Warburton
before the Lions Tour 2013

Giovanni with professional football
legends Aaron Ramsey
and Trevor Sinclair

Giovanni & Martin Bashir

Giovanni & Katherine Jenkins at No.10 Nightclub enjoying Italian style cockles and laverbread

Giovanni with Joe Calzaghe and Frankie Dettori who rides fasta on Giovanni's pasta!

Giovanni with Paul McKenna

Giovanni & José Carreras

Giovanni & his sister Francesca with chef Ainsley Harriott and star Len Goodman

Giovanni and Gareth Edwards

Giovanni and Garry Sobers the first cricketer to hit 6 sixes in an over.

Giovanni with Coronation Street and Loose Women star Denise Welch (& Denise's Dad in the background!)

Giovanni with Italian Rugby Star Mirco Bergamasco and Celebrity Chef Gino Di Campo

Giovanni & Barry Humphries (Dame Edna)

Giovanni & Princess Diana at her charity event with Luciano Pavarotti

Giovanni with Michelle Keegan (Coronation Streets Tina McIntyre)

Write down your greatest memories of times when you ...

Felt positive

_____

_____

_____

_____

_____

_____

_____

Felt confident

_____

_____

_____

_____

_____

_____

_____

Felt outstanding

_____

_____

_____

_____

_____

_____

_____

_____

Achieved something

_____

_____

_____

_____

_____

_____

_____

_____

When was the last time your mind wandered off to somewhere far away? Where did it wander? It's too easy to let our mind stray into negative places. Often, we commiserate over our struggles, bad relationships, and heartache. This inevitably deteriorates our emotional state.

Cooking is a prime time when your mind may go into a trance. The repetitive actions and monotonous aura created when cooking the same typical meal, sends our mind into a spiral of grudging and often hypothetical thoughts. The meal gets cooked, but you can't really remember cooking it. Your loved ones are distant and inconsiderate, not appreciating the meal you have produced. Sound familiar? This book will teach you to use that time in the kitchen to shift your mind into a positive state, as well as creating a delicious, fulfilling meal you can be proud of.

If you find yourself slumping into a negative place, simple turn to the contents page where you will find a number of categories for overcoming different challenges. The points within these categories will assist you in taking the first steps to tackle your challenges. It's all about staying present and enjoying the culinary delights you are creating. This book is your first aid kit in the kitchen. It's your personal possession to help heal you of dark thoughts. If you trust the suggestions in this book, those negative thoughts won't come anywhere near your kitchen. Eventually, they won't come anywhere near you.

Remember to enjoy cooking and visualise the life you deserve. Today can be the first day of that life.

We suggest you make notes on the pages provided in this book for your breakthroughs whilst reading this book. Make this book about you and your journey.

Writing this book is a dream come true. If we can, so can you. What's your dream?

What is the ONION EFFECT?

The **ONION EFFECT** represents what can happen if you allow yourself to go down a spiral of negative thoughts. With every layer peeled off, the smaller the onion becomes until, eventually, there's nothing left, this represents a life problem. This is mirrored when we let one problem take us down a journey of many more. By thinking about the hypothetical consequences of a problem rather than thinking of a solution, you are allowing your mind to peel back your layers until you are in a negative emotional state, or zero energy.

For example, believe it or not, if Giovanni were to see a dirty floor by the front door of his restaurant, the **ONION EFFECT** could take place.

He at times would go into a spiral of negative thoughts. (**1st layer**)

He would believe his restaurants aren't being looked after and therefore will lose his customers. (**2nd layer**)

If the restaurants were to lose their customers, there would be no business. (**3rd layer**)

Without a business, Giovanni would not be able to pay his bills (**4th layer**)

Nor have money for his childrens' future (**5th layer**)

Or be able to live (**6th layer**) and may lose his home and possessions.

With all those layers peeled away, Giovanni has created a negative state of mind and emotions, when all he had to do was simply remind his staff to clean the front.

It is easy to not realise you are doing this until it becomes critical. You are responsible for how low you let yourself go.
As Martyn once told me "keep your emotions out of it"

Think of a time you may have done this, even after hearing the words "what is all the fuss about?".

It's only once you hit rock bottom in that moment that you are able to snap out of it. This is a pure waste of energy. Sadly, some people just can't!

The basis of this book is to lay the foundations for you to make positive changes in your life that will benefit you and your family.

The photos on **page 14 – 15** show a few of the many celebrities that have visited Cardiff and have become accustomed to the authentic Italian dining and fantastic service at Giovanni's restaurants. Celebrities including the late Luciano Pavarotti, Sir Tom Jones and Dame Shirley Bassey are just a few of the many hundreds of celebrities who have dined at Giovanni's.
Giovanni said, we have been looking after celebrities for over 35 years but the real celebrities are his loyal customers his staff and especially his sister Francesca who is the rock of Giovanni's empire.

"meeting and serving celebrities has been inspirational to everybody. I have always treated celebrities as people who never gave up on their dreams and who still deserve privacy and respect when dining".

What is a pattern interrupt?

Consider the statement above. It doesn't really make sense when you think about it!! Are you now distracting yourself from what you were previously thinking about? This is a good way to take someone out of a negative thought pattern and bring them back to the present moment.

So, a pattern interrupt is an action that when followed through can move someone from a negative thought pattern and give them the opportunity to choose a positive thought. Basically, you are more aware of your own thinking patterns and will catch yourself beginning to spiral into a negative pattern and have the ability to alter your thoughts to more positive ways of thinking, bringing better results in the way you feel. This in turn makes you more present and mindful moment by moment, which is paying attention to your thoughts and how they make you feel.

Getting back on track

When you catch yourself spiralling into negative thought patterns, you can either turn off the gas and read the whole book or you can get back to being present and mindful and continue your cooking, Now!! This is a book that you can refer to over and over for recipes and emotional healing.

Any time you feel stuck or catch your mind drifting to unwanted thoughts refer to this is a pattern interrupt!!

Pattern interrupt

Your notes

"Today is the first day of the rest of your life".

Charles Dederich

This book is partly about bringing busy families together around the dining table. It will help rekindle the lost art of communication which has been overtaken by gizmos, gadgets, phones, tablets, and computers. This book presents an opportunity to put down the gadgets, turn off the TV and spend a little time together. Talk, listen, share your experiences and pain. As they say, a trouble shared is a trouble halved. Turn to **page 145** for more information on the positive effects of taking time out for family dining.

Despite the negative consequences of the rise in mobile devices, with the right balance, they can be used for good. If you don't have time to talk, why not text each other more? Text a family member every morning with three things you're grateful for. Every evening, text them three positive things that happened to you that day. This is a great way to keep up with each other's lives, as well as putting yourself in a positive mood before you sleep and before you start your day.

Most of us have all experienced loss, lack of confidence, loneliness, anxiety or depression. This book is a recipe for changing the way you think and the things you do around meal times. These changes will have a positive effect on you and your family.

Showing appreciation for one another is incredibly important for maintaining healthy relationships. If you're not feeling appreciated, acknowledge it and communicate it to them.

In life we all get so busy with our day-to-day lives that we can take for granted our friends and family. This can then turn into grudges being held and arguments being started. The lesson is to acknowledge those around you and if you have a problem, address it and communicate it clearly to those involved.

*"Step up
and make it happen"!*

Giovanni L Malacrino

Tips

Don't hold back, say what you really mean
Very often people don't say what is really going on. If you don't tell the whole story, how can the other person understand?

Speak from your heart, not your head:
When you speak from the heart you are really communicating what you feel about the situation and this gets to the real crux of the matter.

Are you listening with intent?
Make sure you are present to the conversation and really hearing what the other person is trying to say.

Quite often communication breaks down because of an argument. This is a useful metaphor to keep in mind:
When there's a pan fire in the kitchen, there are four types of people.

One person will throw water over the fire, which could actually make it worse.

Another person will take the pan outside, which could potentially burn them.

Another person will panic and run away.

Finally, the responsible person, will use a fire extinguisher or a damp cloth. This is the person who puts the fire out straight away.

These people represent reactions in an argument:

1. **The hothead** – throwing water on the fire is a gut reaction but can fuel the fire. When we respond emotionally with anger and hurt, we can escalate an argument.
2. **The person who holds a grudge** – holding onto the pan will burn you. When we hold on to anger, we are the ones who get hurt.
3. **The person who fears confrontation** – running away from the fire means it can spread and get out of control. The longer we leave dealing with an issue, the greater the problem becomes.
4. **The person we all want to be:** calm, collected, deals with the problem effectively.

When it comes to putting out a feud, communicate effectively, directly, and straight away. Don't give the argument time to fester and grow into something bigger than it really is.

When someone upsets us and we don't communicate our feelings, we are carrying the pain. Follow Steve's tips at the beginning of this section: speak to the person involved and, using the strategies above, have an honest conversation and find the resolution so that you can have closure.

Quite often, when cooking, we go over things we wish we could say, creating trapped emotions and the inability to set these words free takes us to a negative place. Instead, think about what you want to say – then say it. Let your kitchen be your stage to express how you truly feel.

Here are a few tips on how to communicate:

1. Never point the blame, simply express emotions.
2. Be clear and don't rush or you could end up distorting or generalising what you want to say.
3. Focus on the issue, not the person.
4. When they are speaking, pay attention.
5. Never jump to conclusions, listen first.

That last point is extremely important. Have you ever spent hours preparing a meal, only for your partner to turn up late, have already eaten or simply not being considerate of your hard work? If the answer is yes, you'll know how it feels to be slowly simmering yourself to boiling point.

But, consider these:
- Did you let them know you were preparing the meal?
- Did they tell you they might be late?
- Perhaps they had a really awful day?

Remember, communicate your emotions and allow the other person to do the same. No more boiling over, just calm communication of each other's emotions followed by a delicious meal.

Have something you want to get off your chest?
Recently had an argument with somebody that hasn't been discussed or communicated?

Invite them over for a meal and discuss the matter – try our **Six Cheese Pasta Explosion** recipe on **page 116**.

"Life is like baking a cake,
if you have the right ingredients,
it will always turn out well!
Bake it together".

Giovanni and Stephen

It Started with a Fart

A metaphor by Giovanni Malacrino

A couple who have been together for years have fallen out of love, but they are too busy to end their relationship or communicate about it. One day, on their anniversary, they find a spare moment to begin discussing their plans to break up. All the family are coming over to celebrate with gifts, so they decide that now is not the right time to discuss it as it will ruin everyone's mood. They decide to book a table at an Indian restaurant, where they arrive already grumpy with each other.

As the night goes on, they drink more alcohol and eat more delicious food. They begin to forget they hate each other. In fact, they feel closer than ever, holding hands on the walk home. They get home and are so in love that they go straight to bed and make love.

The next morning comes around. They wake to a bright, sunny morning in each other's arms. Then the husband lets out an almighty fart and lifts the covers to smell it. The wife thinks to herself how much she hates it when he does that. She gets up, goes downstairs to get away from him and makes her own breakfast, thinking

"That will teach him to fart in bed."

The husband gets out of bed and notices his wife has only made breakfast for herself. He decides to ignore her during their entire journey to each other's work that will teach her. When the wife finishes work, she decides to go shopping instead of going straight home to cook dinner for them both, to get back at him for ignoring her.

The husband returns home and, finding she's not there, decides to go to the pub. Finally, the wife returns home. As her husband is at the pub, she puts the food in the fridge and goes straight to bed, still extremely angry at him. He eventually returns home with a takeaway for them both, but feeds it to the dog to teach her a lesson when he realises she's gone to bed.

This back-and-forth passive aggressive attitude continues until the next anniversary, when it begins all over again.

Had the wife initially communicated how much she hated her husband farting in bed, he would have apologised there and then. She would have made him breakfast, he wouldn't have ignored her in the car, they would have enjoyed tea together, gone shopping together, enjoyed a drink together at the pub and a takeaway together. If she had said what was on her mind, their love for each other would have lasted.

Focus on the good stuff that's going right and communicate on what's going wrong.

Your notes

Be grateful I am still here:
Invest the energy you spend worrying about getting older into enjoying the here and now instead.

Head for the gym, not the gin:
We can't slow down time, but we can look after ourselves a bit better.

Accept what I cannot change:
Instead of letting fear rule you, embrace life as it is and make the most of the time you do have.

In this world, so many people pass away too young. Those people would love to have the joy of getting older.

Remember: You are as old as you feel! Age is just a number. When you're doing the right things you can feel whatever way you choose.

Follow these steps to feel healthier and happier:
1. Keep yourself supple with daily light stretches
2. Go for a short walk every day
3. Stick to a healthy weight through exercise and a balanced diet
4. Have regular health checks
5. Find at least 10 minutes a day to focus on your breathing. Breathe in as fully as you can. Hold it for as long as you can and release as much as you can. Then repeat.

As we get older we should find we have more time to do important things, and share our knowledge as our life is changing. Many people who have retired wonder how they ever had time to go to work. Now they are enjoying doing things there was no time for when they worked.

Think of something you really love doing. Now do more of it. Think of something you have always wanted to do. Now do it. Now is always the best time to take action. Now is the only guaranteed time you have to make a positive difference in your life. Remember, it's okay.

Eat healthier! Use our **Super Detox Green Smoothie** on **page 138**.

Your notes

"Your eyes are
the gateway to your soul:
Look within yourself
and choose what you want".

Stephen Truelove

Stop comparing myself to others:

When we get caught up in jealousy, we stop seeing the good things in ourselves.

What was the last compliment I had?

Think about a time when someone said something nice about you or when you felt proud of something you accomplished.

Remember you have the power to change.

When you change to a positive mindset and feel good about yourself, your insecurities will disappear, and jealousy will have no power over you.

The first step to tackling jealousy is recognising the green-eyed monster in yourself. Jealousy is something only you can deal with. Begin by thinking about why you are jealous. Is it another person's success? Is it their confidence? Their looks? These are not really the reasons we are jealous. Jealousy is a mirror to what we feel is lacking in our own lives. We become jealous due to our own insecurities, trust issues, inability to feel deserving of something or not being comfortable in our own skin.

The next time you look in the mirror, look straight at yourself. Gaze into your own eyes. You're looking into your soul. Have fun with this. Now, repeat out loud:

"I love and accept myself!"

Ignore the little voice in the back of your head trying to tell you not to love yourself. Say it again if you need to. And again. Keep saying it until you truly begin to believe it. Eventually, jealousy will begin to drain out of your life.

Consider: Cooking a meal for two and sharing your jealous feelings with the person involved. Perhaps you can work through it together to help you let go of the jealous emotion.

Love yourself!
Fill up on vitamin rich foods, good bacteria and improve your well-being. Try our **Sauerkraut** recipe on **page 104**.

Your notes

"Your health is your most precious possession: Look after it, you will be better for it"!

Stephen Truelove

Call a friend and make some plans

Who brings fun and laughter to you most when you are with them?
Make arrangements to meet up with them more often.
Do it now.

Put music on and move your body

Music and dance is a therapy by itself, put on your favourite song and
sing and dance to it, naked if you like! Just have fun.

Remember something that made you, Laugh out loud

What is the funniest thing you have seen or heard?
Replay it in your imagination and get yourself laughing again.
Take a moment to consider the last time you really had fun.
Have you found yourself stuck in a rut? Sometimes we get caught in
the routine of life, full of daily chores. We no longer have time to do
the activities which bring us fun and laughter.

Consider these points:
• What are you going to do to change your daily routine?
• When are you going to make the change?
• What difference will this make?
• How will it affect those around you?

Here's a tip: the answer to the second question is **Now**.
Get off the treadmill (hamsters' wheel) and start doing the things you
enjoy. We are not on this planet for very long, so have fun now.
They say laughter brings healing, so do what you enjoy, laugh more
and feel healthier.

Do you find cooking a chore?

Let's make it more fun.

Follow in the steps of the famous *Friends* character Rachel Green. Her attempt at making a trifle ended up with a concoction of fruit, jam and beef – because the pages of the recipe book were stuck together. Despite sounding disgusting, a certain Joey Tribbiani found it delicious.

Make your own concoction. Get creative, see what you can come up with. Use your imagination: it's limitless.

Cook a hands-on messy meal!
Messy food is fun food! Use our **Panne e Verdure** recipe over on **page 106**.

Your notes

*"The best action to take
is the one that takes you forward"!*

Stephen Truelove

Bite on a wooden spoon or pencil as in the picture above

This sends a message to your brain to release endorphins to help you feel happier, as it's challenging to feel sad whilst smiling.

What was the best time you ever had?

Thinking of the best time puts you in a different state. It's impossible to feel good and sad at the same time.

Whose company do you enjoy most?

I always feel good and happy when I'm with... Think about those good times. Can you arrange to meet them today or tomorrow?

What is the best thing you have ever done?

What is your best achievement that made you feel proud and happy? Think about it and really immerse yourself in that good feeling.

Create great memories

Thinking about great memories can be a therapeutic way to get our minds back on track whilst cooking.

Here's a strategy to incorporate your memories into your food:

1. Think about one of your best memories – those that makes you feel outstanding.
2. Smell some of your favourite herbs and spices whilst thinking of outstanding times.
3. Do this over and over with all your favourite memories.

Eventually, whenever you smell these herbs and spices, those great memories will come flooding back to you. Your cooking preparation is now a time for positive reminiscing and will set you up for a glorious cooking session and a happy mindset.

Build yourself a portfolio of outstanding memories which will come back to you when you cook. To really get the best out of this method, make your memories bigger and brighter. Make the feelings attached to the memories stronger, as if you're re-living the memory for the very first time. Anchor the smells of your favourite aromas.

Check out our aromatic **Trio Di Carne** on **page 132**.

Your notes

"When your power is down
your lights are dim,
When your power is strong
your lights shine bright"!

Stephen Truelove

Re- focus your thoughts, think of something unusual

This will create a distraction that stops the obsessive thought patterns in their tracks.

Make a commitment to yourself and take up a new hobby

When you take up something new or develop an interest, you will focus on it, retraining the brain to think about different things other than your obsession.

Put distance between you and what you're obsessing about

The bigger the distance, the less it is on your mind, giving you a chance to let go of the stranglehold of obsessive thinking. Obsessive thoughts are all-consuming. When a thought creates a feeling which in turn creates a thought and then recreates the feeling and so on. This vicious circle spirals us into negative patterns.

We create our own thoughts, followed by a feeling which then creates the behaviour. When we get into this cycle of thinking and feeling over and over, we are letting ourselves become obsessed with something. Once we are obsessed, the thought and feeling associated with the problem we are focusing on become all-consuming. Obsessions can lead to irrational behaviours, which can play havoc with our emotions and mental state.

Remember, an obsession stems from a thought. But a thought has no power: it is the meaning we put into it that has the impact on our emotional well-being. Take away that meaning and we can begin tackling the obsession.

A quick and easy solution for obsession is to become aware of the feeling created by our thoughts. Recite over and over in your mind:

"This brain is having a thought."

By continuously thinking this, it will override the obsessive thought and keep you present. This is based on the Buddhist technique of attachment and non-attachment to keep you mindful in the moment. With practice and persistence, we can melt away our obsessive thinking.

Take up a new hobby with cooking – with our recipe, **Chicken and Vegetables Stir Fry** over on **page 130**.

Your notes

"*Whatever you don't confront in life, you become the victim of*".

Derek Ayre

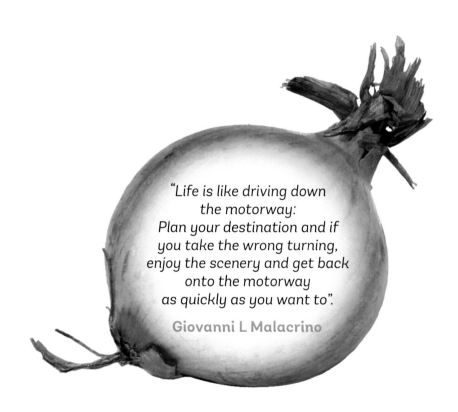

"*Life is like driving down
the motorway:
Plan your destination and if
you take the wrong turning,
enjoy the scenery and get back
onto the motorway
as quickly as you want to*".

Giovanni L Malacrino

Make some time to create a plan

Get a pen and paper and write a list of what you want to achieve for the day or the week ahead.

What do you need to prioritise?

Look at your list and highlight the things that are most important for you to accomplish. Use the colours red, green and amber to prioritise.

What is your time-scale?

Now that you have your list, grab your calendar or diary and set your deadlines to accomplish your tasks.

Often life can become so hectic that we bumble along, hoping things will work out for the best. We have no structure or goals. Planning your life can be a major step in feeling more positive. We have so many activities in life which need planning: meals, trips with friends, meetings with colleagues. Without careful planning, these activities can become burdens of stress.

A simple way to become better at organising is to create your own to-do list and stick to it. We all know how frustrating it is when we forget to take our shopping list to the shop: we end up with unnecessary items and forget the most important things.

On your to-do list, remember to include dates to complete things, who the activity is with and, most importantly, prioritise through colour coordination or set the list in order of importance. Tick off things as you go, and let yourself feel proud of every task accomplished.

Everyone's way of planning is different. Perhaps your mind doesn't work in lists? Try different strategies and find a way that works perfectly for you.

Here is an example template of a planning sheet:

Do it
You'll feel better. Really

Today's goals

1. _____
2. _____
3. _____
4. _____

Must do today

1. _____
2. _____
3. _____
4. _____
5. _____

Be there – Date/time

_____

_____

_____

_____

Do this

_____

_____

_____

_____

_____

_____

_____

_____

_____

Cook this

_____

_____

_____

_____

Make quick meals that don't require a lot of prep or equipment. Recommend you prep the day before and reheat quickly for the following day, as this will give you more time to become more organised in other aspects of your life. Why not arrange an evening for our **Spiced Squash Soup** on **page 100**.

Your notes

"*Beliefs can make you
or break you,
so believe you can,
and you will*".

Stephen Truelove

Consider things from a different perspective
When we step back from a situation, it allows us to see things in different ways.

Learn to let go
If you are holding on to something emotionally, then it is you who is hurting.

Take some responsibility for your part
When we take responsibility for our part in any situation we begin to let go of blame, which is the first step to a resolution.

When you forgive, you heal. As they say, he who holds the hot coals gets burnt! If someone has said or done something which has hurt you and you are still feeling that pain, it's you that is holding on. You are the one who is stuck. When you can truly forgive the person or situation, you can set yourself free.

You don't necessarily have to like what's happened or make up with a particular person, but you do need to learn to forgive. Take your power back and move on. Remember, what goes around comes around.

Think about these points when practising forgiveness:
1. What could you be responsible for with regard to the problem that will enable you to forgive?
2. Who is affected the most by your inability to let go of what you're emotionally holding on to?
3. Write down the emotional feeling you have associated with your inability to forgive – for example, regret or anger.
4. Call the person you have an issue with, tell them you forgive them and put the phone down, this may ease the pain.

Now incorporate these steps into your forgiveness:
1. Forgive yourself.
2. Slow down playing the victim.
3. Stop carrying your negative emotions around with you.
4. Put issues in the past where they belong.

Please go to my YouTube channel and watch my video on forgiveness.
www.youtube.com/c/LovelifeloveyouUk

> **Step back from the situation** – take time out and put your issues in the past. Use our **Farfalle Garrabiata** recipe on **page 112**, it is a more complicated recipe that requires your attention which ensures you're stepping back from the situation you have found yourself in.

Your notes

"Our greatest challenge is not to live the life we lead but to lead the life we want".

Stephen Truelove

Commit yourself

When you want to achieve more in your life, you have to put yourself fully into what you want. What do you enjoy most about what you want to achieve? Start doing what you enjoy and progress from there

Realise your true potential

Take a moment to become aware of your unique talents. When you realise and take ownership of your strengths, then you can develop them to achieve more.

Take action

What's the first step you can take towards what you want to achieve? You can be, do and have whatever you want.

BE

To achieve more, we have to be more committed to our cause. By putting our commitment into action, our achievements can flourish. For example, we can improve something in our lives such as our health. To do this, we would have to commit to a new regime. When you start any new exercise programme, let's say 3 days at the gym or a long walk. In order to succeed with your new plan, think about the skills and attitudes it requires. **For example, would you have to be determined?**

Or motivated? Or more positive? Consider whether this comes naturally to you, or how you would have to prepare yourself to be this way.

DO

Then you have to put things into action. No more excuses. Let's say a programme of exercise or take that long walk. You have to turn up at the gym 3 days a week and do the programme of exercise. That's the doing part. You have now committed to something and you are determined to get healthier.

HAVE

You then have what you want – better fitness, feeling healthier, etc. Use this strategy in any area of your life where you want to achieve more and you really can be, do and have what you want. This method can be adapted for anything we want to achieve: health, happiness, wealth, or being a better communicator.

Now that you have a method to achieve more of what you want in life, which areas will you focus on? We all have the potential to possess what we want in life. When we become committed, things will come to fruition.

Choose what you want to achieve. **Be it, do it and have it.**

What about cooking a difficult meal, practice makes perfect! **Give this a go**, our **Squid Ink Pasta** recipe on **page 110**.

Your notes

"Whether you realise it or not your subconscious mind is your best friend, work with it and it will produce wonderful things for you".

Stephen Truelove

Becoming aware of the name and colour is the start of taking back control of your fear

If that feeling of fear had a name and colour what would they be?
Our minds work in pictures and colours. Becoming aware of the colour is the start of taking control of your fear.

Realise it is just a feeling
Remember it is just a feeling produced from a thought; a thought creates a feeling, which in turn creates the behaviour.

Change the name and colours of the image you have in mind
When you change the name and colours of the image you will begin to feel different about that fear that had been initially attached to that memory and put you in a better state.

Fear stops us in our tracks

It has been said we are born with two innate fears: fear of falling and fear of loud noises. Other fears are learnt through experience and conditioning from others, generally in our first seven years.
For example, a fear of spiders can be learnt through being in the presence of someone else's fearful reaction during our younger years. As we are still developing, we assume this is normal behaviour and take it upon ourselves to act the same way.

Fear is usually recognised as a feeling in our body similar to nervousness. If there is nothing in our environment at the time to trigger any sort of fear, it can be brought on by something we are thinking about, which is often outside of our awareness. This is the same with many of our emotions. This is our thoughts creating our fears. Our mind works in pictures, and sometimes experiences from our past have not been fully processed through the mind. These thoughts can get stuck in a cycle which can be triggered through one of our five senses. Some experiences can become exaggerated in our internal representation. By using the method above, we can alleviate the feeling of fear. This will leave us more empowered and able to move past our fears.

Cook something you've never tried before! Our octopus recipe will be perfect! Head over to **page 118** to cook up **Seared Scallops and Baby Octopus served with Samphire**.

Five senses VAKOG:
Visual, Auditory, Kinesthetic, Olfactory, Gustatory.

Your notes

"*Dreams never die,
they just get put on hold*".
Giovanni L Malacrino

What are the best compliments you have ever had?

What are the five nicest things anyone has said about you?

What are your best assets?

Focus on your good points. What part of you do you love best?

Why compare yourself to others?

Accept how you are. Other people have their own insecurities. When we compare with someone else, they usually have something we don't have. If you recognise this, then work on getting it for yourself.

We all go through life with insecurities. We compare ourselves with others, measuring our flaws alongside their strengths.

We can encounter different types of insecurities, including:

Social insecurities

This type of insecurity can make you feel anxious about social situations. Social insecurities can develop an internal fear within us of being rejected or disliked by others.

Ask yourself what was the best comment I got on an evening out?

Professional insecurities

Being insecure about your professional life is mainly displayed through a fear of not being able to do or losing your job.

Ask yourself what was the last thing I achieved in my work and got praised for? NB Remember to praise yourself and not wait for others.

Economic insecurities

A fear you may have a shortage of money at some point in your life or your money is not being spent or invested wisely.

Create a new savings and spoil myself account, even if you put a small amount in each month. It will bring security to have fun with and create magic moments.

Personal insecurities

This area of insecurity is the most saturated. Personal insecurities can cover your marital status and also your relationship status with friends, relatives and others.

In whose company do I feel good about myself?

What's different when I'm with them?

Insecurities can be due to uncertainty, self-doubt or lack of something in your life. Uncertainty creates lack of confidence. As you build your confidence, you become more sure of yourself and your insecurities will subside.

Awareness

Realising what area of your life your insecurities are in is a good starting point to resolving them.

Why do you doubt yourself in certain situations?

Why do you not feel good enough or deserving of something?

Share

When you share that your feeling insecure and what you're insecure about with someone close, you can then discuss ways of finding solutions to resolve the challenge that is causing the feeling of insecurity. Sometimes support from someone neutral to your challenge will allow you to let go of your insecurity.

Methods to feel more secure

Spend some time with someone close who knows you well and you can trust. Take turns to write down your values in life, your good points, your achievements and what you really love about yourself. This will help you focus on the good things and build self-esteem, confidence and a more secure feeling in yourself.

Build your confidence with a friend you trust and love, invite them over for a meal to discuss your insecurities. Our recommended meal for a friend's night in would be our **Surf 'n' Turf Steak with Shrimp** recipe over on **page 134**.

Your notes

"*Take control of your own life, embrace positivity and ignore negativity*".

Giovanni L Malacrino

Change your physiology

You will benefit from doing it sooner rather than later.

What will you lose if you don't complete the task.
The reason I started procrastinating in the first place is…

Let's try something different

Let's set the scene, today is Monday. Your deadline for your task is next Friday. Complete it by Wednesday, or even better delegate it.

How does that feel?

Procrastination can be a way of putting yourself under pressure. Some people thrive at putting things off until the last minute and then it's one mad rush to get it done.
It's an adrenaline rush that some enjoy and others hate?

Procrastination often gets created through our experiences during our early years of development. If we have learnt to put things off, then we need to understand the reason behind it.
How long have you practised procrastinating?

Can you trace back in your memory to when you began the habit of procrastinating?

Was it because you got something emotionally fulfilled by leaving things until the last minute or was it because of something experienced in a good way so you try to reproduce it, or in a bad way so you try to avoid it?

Generally when we find the reason we began the practice of procrastinating then we can choose a better way so we no longer put things off.

Procrastination can also stem from fear: fear of failing, fear of making mistakes or fear of success. Fear stops you from achieving more. If it is a fear, identify your fear and you can learn to stop procrastinating. To tackle your fears, refer to **page 59**.

What is it that's stopping you from doing the things you keep putting off?
Is it fear or do you get some sort of kick out of it.

For some people, being told what to do by someone else is frustrating or annoying. The defensive part of them rebels by specifically not doing what they've been told to do. For others, the adrenaline rush when working under pressure gives them an enjoyable high and produces a better outcome. After every high, however, there is generally a low. What goes up must come down.

Don't put it off, get it done! Don't put off any recipes in this book, cook them all, try them all and get them ticked off!
Try something exciting like our **Seafood Medley** on **page 122**.

Your notes

"Love can be expensive, both when you meet and when you part. Communicate, be honest and see what happens".

Giovanni L Malacrino

Dance your funniest dance
Wave your arms and legs around and wiggle your body.

What are your happiest memories?
Close your eyes and remember your happiest times and get that great feeling back.

What makes you laugh out loud?
What is the funniest thing you can think of that makes you laugh so much your belly hurts?

We are all searching for happiness in life. But, happiness can't be found on the outside, it's something we feel inside ourselves.

How can you be happier in many more areas of your life, such as health, happiness and success?
The truth is only you yourself can make you truly happy and generally it's how you think about things.

What can you change in your life, so you become happier?
Many people are looking for something or someone to make them happier. The way you think creates the way you feel and then causes your behaviours. Start being more aware of your thoughts so you choose better ones which creates better feelings and then more productive behaviours making you happier.

Remember your thoughts create your feelings which in turn create your behaviours. Change your mindset change your life. You can be happier when you choose to. When something you do or someone you spend time with helps you feel happier, do more of it.

Happiness strategy anchor!
1. Think of your happiest memories.
2. Visualise the picture of one of your happiest memories.
3. Hear the sounds that you heard at that time.
4. Make your happy feelings twice as strong.
5. When that feeling of happiness is at its strongest, squeeze your ear lobe, and repeat.

Do this exercise over and over until whenever you touch your ear, you instantly get that happy feeling.

You have now anchored!!

Invite somebody that makes you smile over and make them smile with our delicious **Pasta Alla Frutta** recipe on **page 108**.

Your notes

"The difference between frustration and disappointment is as follows. Frustration means there still time to do something about it. Disappointment means it's too late".

Giovanni L Malacrino

What am I grateful for?

When was the last time your partner did something nice for you that made you smile?

Make a list.
When was the last time you and your partner did something nice together that made you both smile?

Let go of your fear and have fun together

Walk in the rain, go barefoot in the sand and roll in the grass.

Value yourself even more

Love and accept yourself the way you are after all why not?

We should do things for someone because we love them or we love doing things for them. True love can dissolve many hurts, unconditional love can move many mountains. Feel an abundance of love as your cooking a meal for you and your loved ones and don't get lost in your own negative thoughts.

What love and emotion are you normally in when you're cooking?

We all have a conscious and subconscious mind. When you are focussed on what you are doing, you could say you are cooking consciously. When you are not present and lost in your own thoughts you are not being productive. That is when your emotions can spill over and cause un-easiness within you and create issues in relationships.

You choose how you love and how you feel. It is a fact that your emotions can affect your energy and your taste buds.

Negative energy can put negativity into your love life and into your food. So next time your cooking be aware of how positive you are feeling. Only cook from love and notice how your food tastes better.

Never cook or eat when your angry

Cook a romantic meal for your loved one, we suggest our
Peppered Steak with Creamy Mushroom Sauce on **page 128.**

Your notes

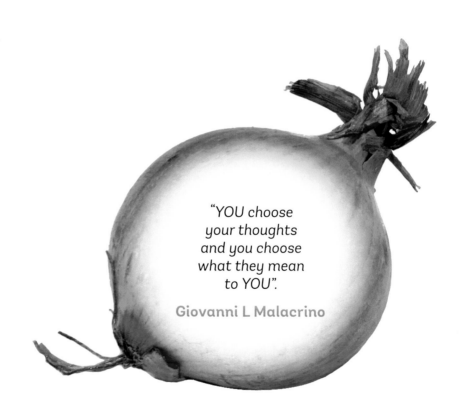

*"YOU choose
your thoughts
and you choose
what they mean
to YOU".*

Giovanni L Malacrino

Look for the good in yourself:

When you focus on the great things you do. You appreciate the difference you make to others.

Write a list of why you want to be appreciated

Write a letter of why you want to be appreciated. Give it to those concerned and expect a letter back. This is the start of better communication.

Appreciation equals value:

How much do you really value yourself?

Most people just want some appreciation for nice things they do for others. Some notification that what you do isn't taken completely for granted. Those who do things from love or just because you want things to be easier and better for others and have learned to do it just because you want to without looking for anything in return will already have self-appreciation.

When we do things for something in return then we are usually trying to create an outcome – i.e. if I do this nice thing for them, then they will tell me what I want to hear so I feel better about myself – then there is something missing for ourselves and that can be self-appreciation.

Start by communicating how you don't feel appreciated and then work on appreciating yourself because if you don't appreciate yourself others may forget. When you learn to appreciate yourself then the need for appreciation from others won't seem as important. Focus on what you appreciate about yourself and the things you do especially for others, do unconditionally.

Give yourself some praise, you don't have to wait for others. When you look at yourself in the mirror, do you see someone who appreciates themselves? Love and appreciate yourself fully and then others will show their appreciation for you. Start by looking in the mirror as before, only this time look into your eyes and say

"I completely and fully appreciate myself " and listen to what the conversation is that comes back in your self-talk.

Continue to do this exercise and soon you will learn to appreciate yourself, and though it will still be nice to be appreciated by others, it won't bother you so much when you're not.

Share your list with loved ones around the dinner table!
Use our **Chickpea Cauliflower Curry on Spicy Quinoa** recipe for the perfect dinner guest meal – head over to **page 102.**

Your notes

*"We become our thoughts.
Be careful what you think"!*

Stephen Truelove

I used to be more decisive but now I'm not so sure!

Stop over-thinking:

Take five minutes to calm your mind with some deep breathing. Write or draw the things that are preventing you from making that decision.

Don't decide, just choose:

Children don't make decisions, they just choose. Trust your inner child and from now on choose instead of deciding, you can always change your mind later.

Stick to your decision

Trust yourself and the choices you make.

Many people struggle when it comes to making a decision about something, whether it's something they want to have or something they want to do.

There is an uncertainty of the consequences that may happen if the decision they make means something doesn't turn out well. The problem we have when we make decisions is the need to justify or back up why we have decided the way we have, and that causes the uncertainty.

Some people are able to make decisions immediately, others will ponder over which way to decide, and others just can't or never seem to be able to decide something.

How do we learn to make better decisions? By making decision making easier!

What if we made a choice instead of a decision? What do we mean by this?

Let's say we have a bowl of pasta and a pizza. How do you decide which one you want?

(See **page 108** for the **pasta recipe**).

Exercise: Decision v. Choice

Say to yourself out loud

"I choose --------- (pick between the pasta and pizza)

because------------"

What's your because?

Is it pasta because it tastes better than pizza? Then that is a decision, because you have a reason for it based on past experience; your mind has gone on a search to decide which one you prefer, and why.

Keep writing and saying this exercise out loud as above until you exhaust all the reasons why you decided to pick one over the other.

Eventually you will arrive at the answer shown in this book (**page 151**). But before you look at the answer, keep doing the exercise until you have no further answers and see if you get the same as will be revealed. Then you will find you make choices instead of decisions, and that is why choices are better than decisions and the process becomes easier and less tedious.

Your notes

*Nothing in the universe
can stop you
when your power within is pure!*

Stephen Truelove

What are you passionate about?

Often when people follow their passion, their purpose follows on from it.

What is important to you?

When you focus on what's really important, you may find a desire that leads you to your purpose.

What makes you feel happiest?

If something or someone helps you feel happiest in yourself, then maybe your purpose lies there?

Many people will ask themselves this question at some point in their lives:

What Is My Purpose?

What do I want to do with my life or what do I want from my life?

A better question might be:
What can I do with my time that is important?

Whatever feels right and important can be what your purpose is. For some, having a purpose gives their lives direction and meaning instead of bumbling along through life just taking things as they come. Your purpose can be what you want it to be.

It can be big or small, it can be clarity around what's important or unimportant in the world. It can be living a life of meaning like following a passion or helping to make a difference to others less fortunate than ourselves.

Let's flip the coin:

Do we really need a purpose?
For some, the answer is probably "**Yes**", but some people may not want a purpose and yet others may be unsure. Let us consider if you are living a healthy and happy life; could that be the purpose of this existence? To enjoy everything you can, to be as healthy as you can, and to be as happy as you can on your journey of life.

Some people have a purpose in life and others don't think they need it.

It's not what you want in life it's why you want it.
With every decision you make.
Ask yourself why before you make it.

Work out what your purpose in life is. Get a pen and answer the following questions:

1. What do you do that makes you smile?
2. What could you do differently?
3. What inspires you?
4. What energises you?
5. What is your biggest lesson so far?
6. Why do you do what you do?
7. Who do you do them for?
8. What are your un-limiting beliefs?
9. How can you be your best?
10. What legacy can you leave behind?

What is your purpose in life?
Give it some thought and write it down. See examples on opposite page.

Whilst answering the questions, why not enjoy our delicious **Power Breakfast Smoothie recipe** on **page 140.**

Your notes

My purpose in life is to learn and help teach others how to live, love, laugh and grow whilst making an abundance of money to share with others.

Giovanni L Mallacrino

My purpose in life is to be outstanding in all areas and excel in health, happiness and success. To motivate and inspire hundreds of thousands of people to achieve their dreams and live their lives to the full while being the best they can be and making a difference to others.

Stephen Truelove

Why are you feeling lonely?

Write down the reasons, now cross them out.

What must you do to stop feeling lonely?

Put on a motivational song and start writing. Visualise yourself not feeling lonely. Close your eyes and imagine yourself doing the things you want.

What can you do to feel better

Phone and visit a friend.

Put on music that motivates you and dance baby dance.

Love and accept yourself the way you are as there are people out there that wish they were you.

No need to feel lonely

Many people like their own company and spending time by themselves. That's being a loner. Loners tend to have special personality traits and don't mind being alone. Loners have good self-worth, are loyal in friendship and never crave the company of others. Loners understand themselves perfectly and have respect for their boundaries and those of others. Loners are strong in difficult situations and when alone will self-reflect.

Though they may get overwhelmed in stressful situations, they will not waste time on distractions and will use alone time for recharging and finding solutions to cope in various situations. Loners are very aware of their thoughts and emotions because of their self-awareness which is an important part of being able to work through and learn from discouraging thoughts and feelings. Time is something they value and respect for themselves and others, so they will nearly always be on time for appointments. Loners have self-respect.

From a NLP (Neuro Linguistic Programming) perspective, if someone is good or successful at something, you can learn how they think and behave in ways that bring them success and then you can have the same results. If you have been living with loneliness, which is generally created through your thoughts and feelings, then you can learn the traits of the loner, which will be the first step to no more lonely feelings and stepping into some of the positive behaviours described above.

Many people don't like being on their own, but there is a difference between being on your own and feeling lonely. If you are comfortable with your own company, that's fine. A basic need in life is connection, which is contact with others and being understood, socializing. If you are missing out on connecting with others, you can take on a new hobby, go to some classes; find a way so you're interacting with other people. You could volunteer your services to help others who may be less fortunate than yourself; there are many organisations and charities who welcome volunteers who make such a huge difference to others' lives.

If you are someone who feels loneliness even in a crowded room, then you can seek out someone who will help you understand why you feel this way. Very often when people realise why they have this feeling and how they are maintaining it, then they are able to resolve the feeling: this puts them in a better place to enjoy the company of others, socialise better and also feel more comfortable by themselves. **Is that something you want?**

Host a dinner party and 'wow' guests with our **Salmon and Shrimp Tempura** recipe on **page 124.**

Your notes

"*If limiting beliefs hold us back,
why not change your beliefs
and un-limit yourself?*

Stephen Truelove

Say " Thank you","" Thank you", "Thank you" for everything you are grateful for in your life

By saying thank you for everything great in your life, you will then attract more wonderful things to be grateful for.

What are your rules in life in order to be grateful?

When you appreciate what you already have in your life, more things for you to appreciate will be drawn to you.

What's great in your life right now?

Make a list of all the great things in your life right now. When you put your energy into doing this, you are creating more great things to flow into your life. Energy flows where focus goes.

Gratitude is a great habit to get into. The more grateful you become for anything great in your life, the more it seems to show up. Move your focus of attention to anything great in your life that you are grateful for and see how that has a positive impact on your day-to-day living. What a great habit. Studies have shown that children who are taught to be grateful experience better things as they grow up.

We need to set the example of good practices to those around us and this is one of the best. People take things and people for granted instead of showing gratitude. Make being grateful a daily habit. Share in turn with each other around the table at meal times three things you are grateful for from your life today, and watch magic things begin to happen over time as you make gratitude a part of your family's daily life. I am so grateful you are reading this.

Need to thank somebody in your life? Invite them over and cook them our delicious **Seafood on a bed of Laverbread** meal on **page 120 –** what better way to say thank you than with a great meal!

Your notes

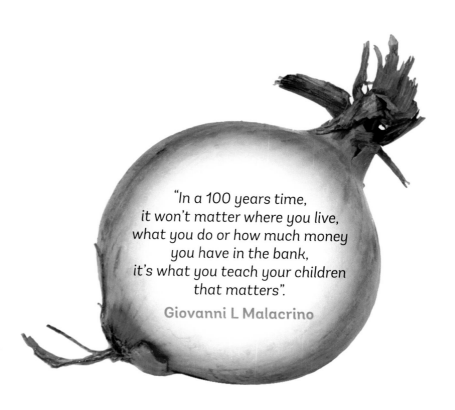

"In a 100 years time,
it won't matter where you live,
what you do or how much money
you have in the bank,
it's what you teach your children
that matters".

Giovanni L Malacrino

Stop!
Take 10 minutes to relax. Take deep breaths and ask yourself do I need this clutter in my life?

Choose three items you haven't used for six months
Either use them, sell them, give them or throw them away.

Find somewhere you want to declutter
Now pick an area and start the process of keeping, selling, giving or throwing away and make some clear spaces.

How does that feel?
As you start to declutter your mind will feel free.

Bedroom, kitchen, living room, cupboards, wardrobes?
Cluttered rooms mean a cluttered mind, so they say.

When you clean up on the outside, it gives more clarity on the inside. It has been suggested that if we keep something for six months or more without looking at it or using it then we don't need it anymore?

Some people keep or hoard things for reasons they are not aware of. It can be emotional attachment that's deeply ingrained from some experience in our lives. Once you start to declutter or sort out it will get easier and you will feel better.

It is true when you think about it, how many times have you put off clearing clutter out but then something happens in your life and you start decluttering, big time.
What are you waiting for? Get cleaning or decluttering!

Make a quick and easy one pan meal with our **Chicken and Vegetable Stir Fry** over on **page 130**.

"We come into this world,
we leave this world,
so make it your choice
to be as happy as
you can in between".

Stephen Truelove

Take ownership of yourself

When you take ownership of yourself, you learn to have control over the outcomes in your life.

What are you responsible for?

Before you push any blame onto someone else regarding a situation you find yourself in, it's worth considering what you can be responsible for regarding the situation first.

Be more aware of what you do and say and feel

When you are more aware of your actions and what you say, you create the opportunity for improvement.

Whenever you point the finger of blame at someone else, remember three fingers are pointing straight back at you. You are choosing the emotion that is being triggered within yourself. It may be triggered by something or someone else, but it is still your choice to feel it and act from it. Being responsible will allow you to be more aware of yourself. In turn, you will master the ability to tackle negative feelings and react in more positive ways in many more situations than before.

I (Steve) took a relationship course where I was asked the question,

"Out of 100%, in your personal relationship, how much percentage are you responsible and how much percentage is your partner responsible, for the relationship to work well?"

What would you say to answer that?

My answer was 50% me and 50% my partner, right?
I was told *"no, you are 100% responsible!"*

After a little shouting and screaming,
"well if I am 100% responsible where does that leave the other person in the relationship?"

Answer: they also are 100% responsible.
That will give any relationship a 200% chance of being better. Makes sense. When you become 100% responsible for yourself in anything you are relating to, then you will see how things begin to improve in many wonderful ways.

What are you waiting for?
Take responsibility 100% for your life, your behaviours and your choices, and make your life a better experience.

Sit down and take time to think about your actions and what you say. Our **Risotto Di Mare Nero** recipe is the perfect recipe to relax to, eat and contemplate, **page 126**.

2020 COMPETITION
(One winner a month throughout 2020)
For a chance to win a supreme cooking experience in Giovanni's school of hospitality and a signed copy of The Therapy of Cooking.

After reading this book, how did it inspire you? What life challenges would you like us to write about in our next edition of The Therapy of Cooking and what are your favorite ingredients so Giovanni can design new recipes for our next edition.

Winners will be selected and informed To enter go to www.giovannismondo.com

In this case, a mother comes home after a full day at work and starts tidying the house and cleaning up the bedrooms as well as putting everything away as usual.

The importance of communicating properly

Your notes

Recipes

These are just a few delicious recipes with a variety of different ingredients to feed your soul.

Links

Launch of Giovanni Malacrino's YouTube channel
https://youtu.be/ʒlpH-MxofCs

What's The Language Of Love - Italian Or French? | First Dates
https://youtu.be/E6vFp-0KO6E

Beetroot Risotto

Cooking tip

To get your risotto texture just right, use the Smear Test. Take a grain of rice and smudge it onto a dark surface. You're aiming to see a bit of the white in the middle but not too much, and also for it to be tender but not be so overcooked it doesn't smudge.

Allergies

Lactose

Intolerances

Dairy

You will need

- Olive oil
- 1 large red onion, peeled and finely chopped
- 2 garlic cloves, peeled and finely chopped
- 250g arborio rice
- 300g cooked beetroot
- 200g grated carrots
- 200g frozen peas
- Handful of mint, finely chopped
- 200g feta cheese
- Sea salt
- Black pepper

Equipment

- Saucepan
- Wooden spoon

Recipe: Thanks to Fay Hansen.

Cooking method

1. Add olive oil to a saucepan and heat up on a high temperature.
2. Sauté the onions in the pan until they are soft.
3. Add ⅔ of the chopped up beetroot to the pan, stirring into the onions and oil.
4. With the rest of the beetroot, create a purée by blending or mixing with a fork – this will be used later.
5. Leave to simmer for a few moments, before adding the rice.
6. Mix the rice well into the pan and leave the risotto to cook for a few minutes.
7. Continue by adding stock to the risotto in small amounts. Continue doing this until the rice is soft and tender, making sure to stir the ingredients continuously.
8. Season to taste with salt and pepper.
9. Stir, stir, and stir.
10. After a few minutes of cooking, add the chopped up mint leaves.
11. Pour in the puréed beetroot, and continue stirring.
12. As the rice is beginning to soften, mix the grated carrots and frozen peas into the risotto.
13. Add a splash of stock, to ensure the vegetables cook.
14. Leave to cook for 3 minutes.
15. Add the feta cheese in small chunks and stir into the risotto.
16. Continue cooking until the risotto has lost most of its liquid, and is a happy medium between a runny and a thick consistency.
17. Serve in a bowl, garnished with feta cheese and mint.

Spiced Squash Soup

Allergies
Nuts, Celery

Intolerances
Citrus, Fruits

Equipment
- Saucepan
- Wooden spoon
- 1 Food blender

You will need
- 1 tsp ground cumin
- 1 tsp ground coriander
- 1 tsp curry powder
- 1 tsp ground turmeric
- 600g butternut squash
- ½ small onion, peeled
- 1 tbsp olive oil
- ¼ red chilli, de-seeded
- 1 tsp finely chopped ginger
- 2 stalks of celery, chopped
- 1 carrot
- 400ml coconut milk
- 200ml hot vegetable stock
- 1 tbsp fresh lime juice
- Pinch of black pepper
- Crushed almonds to garnish

Recipe: Thanks to Fay Hansen.

Cooking method

1. Add olive oil to a saucepan and heat up on a high temperature.
2. Once oil is hot, sauté the chopped onion slices.
3. Next, stir in the finely chopped ginger, turmeric, cumin, coriander, curry powder and red chilli slices. Heat until fragrant.
4. After about 5 minutes, or when the onions begin to soften, add the celery and chopped butternut squash to the pan.
5. Next, add the chopped carrots, followed by the stock.
6. Season with salt and pepper to taste.
7. Simmer on a medium heat for 20 minutes.
8. When the vegetables are beginning to soften, add the contents of the pan to a blender.
9. Begin blending the ingredients together.
10. Pour in the coconut milk and lime juice as the ingredients begin to liquefy.
11. Continue blending until the soup is a creamy consistency.
12. Pour the soup into a bowl and sprinkle with crushed almonds.
13. Garnish with diced coriander leaves.
14. Serve.

"Who are you"?
"Do you know who you really are"?
"And what is your real purpose in life"?

Giovanni L Malacrino

Allergies
Nuts

Intolerances
N/A

You will need
For Cauliflower curry:
- 2 tbsp coconut oil
- 3 tbsp medium curry paste
- 1 tbsp grated fresh ginger root
- 2 large onions, sliced
- ½ cauliflower
- 200g chickpeas
- 400ml coconut milk
- 210ml hot vegetable stock
- 1 tbsp tamari
- 250g green beans
- 1 tbsp cumin seeds
- 1 tbsp tamarind paste

You will need
For Spicy Quinoa:
- 200g quinoa
- 1 ½ tbsp olive oil
- ½ onion diced
- 1 tbsp grated fresh ginger root
- 1 tbsp turmeric
- 1 tbsp coriander
- 75g fresh or frozen peas
- Crushed almonds to garnish •
Salt an pepper

Equipment
- Saucepan
- Wooden spoon
- Frying pan

Recipe: Thanks to Fay Hansen.

Cooking method

Chickpea cauliflower curry

1. Add coconut oil to a saucepan and heat up on a high temperature.
2. Once the oil is hot, add the onions and the curry paste. Cook for 5 minutes.
3. Next, stir in the grated ginger root, followed by the tamarind and cumin seeds. Mix the ingredients together and continue to cook on a medium heat.
4. Spoon in the chickpeas and cauliflower.
5. Pour the stock and coconut milk into the saucepan and drizzle over some tamari.
6. Leave to simmer for 30 minutes, or until the cauliflower is soft, on a low to medium heat.
7. Once the cauliflower is soft, add the chopped green beans and stir into the liquid.
8. Leave to cook for a further 5 minutes.

Spicy Quinoa

1. Add olive oil to a frying pan.
2. Fry the onions with ginger, turmeric and coriander until soft.
3. Once the onions are almost cooked, add the quinoa.
4. Cook altogether for one minute, while continuously stirring.
5. Add the peas.
6. Season with salt and pepper to taste.

- Serve altogether with the chickpea cauliflower curry poured over the top of the spicy quinoa.
- Sprinkle with crushed almonds.
- Garnish with coriander leaves.

You will need

For Spicy Quinoa:
- 2 large carrots, shredded
- 1 medium cabbage, grated
- 2 cabbage leaves, ungrated
- 2 cloves garlic, crushed
- 15g salt (iodine free)

Equipment
- Jam jar
- 1ltr glass jar
- Plastic lid with airlock
- Scales
- Large bowl

Did you know
The brine is created from the salt. It pulls the water out of the cabbage and carrots to create an environment where the good bacteria (lactobacillus) can grow and kill off bad bacteria.

Allergies
N/A

Intolerances
N/A

Recipe: Thanks to Cheryl Hicks.

Cooking method

1. Put grated cabbage, carrots and garlic into the large bowl. Sprinkle over with salt.

2. Use your hands to massage the ingredients together, so you can hear the vegetables crunching. Do this for several minutes, or until the vegetables are squeezing out a substantial amount of liquid.

3. Use your hands to pack the moist vegetables into the jar. Push it right down so it is squished in.

4. Pour the leftover brine into the jar.

5. Use a kraut pounder to push the cabbage down until you can see lots of liquid formed on the top.

6. Cover the top of the Sauerkraut with the cabbage leaves above the water line

7. Put the jam jar on top of the Sauerkraut and seal with the airlock lid.

8. Ferment for 1 – 2 weeks in an 18 – 23 degrees centigrade temperature location. The colder the storage, the longer it will take to ferment.

"Don't worry what others are saying, focus on your truth".

Giovanni L Malacrino

Allergies
Gluten, Lupin, Nuts, Lactose

Intolerances
Dairy

You will need
- 1 loaf of bread

For the courgette spaghetti
- Olive oil
- Salt
- Pepper
- 400g peeled tomatoes
- 75g grated parmesan
- 75g Dolcelatte blue cheese
- 4 medium sized courgettes

For the verdure
- Olive oil
- Salt
- Pepper
- 80g butter
- 2 cloves of sliced garlic
- ½ chopped onion
- ½ chopped red onion
- 1 yellow pepper
- 10 three colours cherry tomatoes
- 1 red chilli
- Pine nuts
- 1 bunch of basil

Equipment
- Sauté Pan
- Serving spoon
- Sharp knife
- Spiralizer

(serves 4 people)

Cooking method

1. Begin spiralizing your courgettes to make courgette spaghetti.
2. Heat sauté pan with a splash of olive oil.
3. Season with salt and pepper.
4. Add the courgette spaghetti.
5. Leave to fry for a minute.
6. Add the peeled tomatoes.
7. Season with salt and pepper.
8. Add the cheeses (parmesan and Dolcelatte blue cheese).
9. Ready to serve.

In another sauté pan

1. Melt the butter with a splash of olive oil.
2. Add the sliced garlic followed by the two sliced half onions.
3. Gently pan fry.
4. Add the yellow pepper.
5. Add the sliced chilli and basil
6. Season with salt and pepper.
7. Finished up with the sliced cherry tomatoes.
8. Empty the inside of the bread loaf.
9. Fill the bread with the courgette spaghetti.
10. Top with the vegetable mix.
11. Decorate with pine nuts and a couple of basil leaves.
12. Ready to serve.

Pasta Alla Frutta

Allergies
Gluten, Nuts, Lactose

Intolerances
Dairy

You will need
- 100g penne pasta
- 50g butter
- 50g raspberries
- 50g blackberries
- 50g blueberries
- 50g strawberries
- 1 lemon
- 1 orange
- 5 leaves of basil
- 25cl Cointreau
- 100g pine nuts
- 100g grated coconut
- 100ml coconut juice
- 125ml of fresh cream
- Salt and pepper

Equipment
- Sauté pan
- 1 saucepan

Cooking method

For the pasta

1. Bring the water to boil.

2. Add salt to season.

3. Cook the pasta till al dente.

4. Drain the pasta.

5. Cool the pasta down with cold water.

When the pasta is cold

1. Add the cream, the pine nuts, the grated coconut and the coconut juice.

2. Stir all the ingredients together.

For the fruit

1. Melt the butter in the frying pan.

2. Add the fruits one by one.

3. Cook on gentle heat for a couple of minutes.

4. Stir in the juice of half a lemon and half an orange.

5. Add the basil leaves.

6. Season with cracked pepper.

7. Add the Cointreau.

8. Cook for a further two minutes.

To serve

1. The pasta will be at the bottom and the fruit will be served hot on top of the pasta.

2. Finish with a sprinkle of grated coconut.

Squid Ink Pasta

Allergies
Fish, Lactose, Gluten

Intolerances
Dairy, Wine

You will need
- Salt
- 100g squid Ink
- 400g spaghetti
- 50g butter
- 1 garlic clove, peeled and chopped
- ¼ red chilli, diced
- 1 tbsp chopped fresh basil leaves
- Salt and pepper
- A dash of white wine

Equipment
- Saucepan
- Frying pan
- Sharp knife
- Wooden spoon
- Colander

Cooking method

1. Add water to the saucepan and bring to the boil.
2. Sprinkle with a pinch of salt.
3. Hold your spaghetti with each hand at each end and break in half. Then, add to the boiling water.
4. Cook the spaghetti until it is al dente.
5. Drain the spaghetti lightly and put to one side.
6. Add butter to a frying pan and heat on a hot temperature until melted, making sure it doesn't burn.
7. Add garlic, red chilli and basil to the pan and stir into the hot butter.
8. Season with salt and pepper.
9. Once the ingredients are submerged in the butter, drizzle it with some olive oil.
10. Leave to cook for a minute on a medium heat.
11. Spoon in the squid ink.
12. Pour over the white wine.
13. Spread evenly across the frying pan and leave to cook for a further minute.
14. Add the drained spaghetti and use a large spoon to mix into the squid ink sauce.
15. Dish a bowl up of the squid ink pasta and garnish with basil leaves.
16. Serve.

"*Believe you are doing amazing and see what happens*".

Giovanni L Malacrino

Farfalle Garrabiata

Cooking tip
If the mixture isn't moist enough when blending, add more milk in small amounts.

Allergies
Gluten, Lactose, Nuts

Intolerances
Dairy, Wine

You will need
- 10g basil leaves
- Olive oil
- 2 tbsp garlic, finely chopped
- 30g pine nuts
- 10g ground black pepper
- 10g salt
- 200g parmesan cheese
- ½ red chilli, finely sliced
- 300ml single cream
- 350g farfalle pasta
- 100g salted butter

Equipment
- Saucepan
- Blender
- Knife
- Chopping board
- Strainer
- Saucepan
- Frying pan
- Large spoon

Cooking method

1. Add water to a saucepan and bring to the boil, before adding a pinch of salt.

2. Once boiling, add your farfalle pasta.

3. Begin preparing your ingredients: Use a sharp knife to finely chop your garlic cloves and red chilli and peel the leaves off the basil.

4. Add the garlic, pine nuts, black pepper, salt, parmesan cheese, chilli, cream and ⅔ of the basil leaves to the blender. Begin blending.

5. Add a splash of olive oil just as the mixture starts to liquefy and continue blending until a creamy consistency.

6. In a frying pan, add a splash of olive oil and your slab of butter and begin melting it.

7. Once it is completely melted, drain your pasta and add it to the butter.

8. Pour your creamy Garrabiata into the pasta and leave to simmer of a medium heat for 2 minutes.

9. Finely cut the rest of your basil leaves and add to the pan. Cook for a further minute, then serve with a sprinkle of parmesan cheese.

"Every situation, properly perceived, becomes an opportunity".

Giovanni L Malacrino

Allergies
Gluten, Lactose

Intolerances
Dairy

You will need

- 5 garlic cloves
- ½ red chilli, finely sliced
- 50g basil leaves
- 150g red cabbage
- 150g mixed peppers
- 150g asparagus
- Salt
- Pepper
- Purple kale
- 4 tomatoes, quartered
- 100g beetroot
- Olive oil
- 300g rigatoni pasta
- 50g salted butter

Equipment

- Blender
- Saucepan

Cooking method

1. Add water to the saucepan and bring to the boil. Once boiling, add your rigatoni pasta.

2. While the pasta is cooking, begin making the sauce. Add 4 garlic cloves to the blender and blend for 10 seconds, or until crushed into small pieces.

3. Next, add half of your finely sliced red chilli, ⅔ of the basil leaves, purple kale, mixed peppers, asparagus, tomatoes and beetroot to the blender. Add a sprinkle of salt and pepper. Begin blending.

4. Once the ingredients begin to liquefy, pour in a splash of olive oil. Continue blending for 5 minutes, or until a creamy, smooth consistency.

5. Once it is al dente, drain your pasta.

6. Add a splash of olive oil to a saucepan and add chopped basil leaves and the rest of your crushed garlic and red chilli.

7. Add the rigatoni pasta to the pan, followed by the creamy sauce. Leave to simmer on a high heat for 2 minutes, stirring occasionally.

8. Add some stock and leave to simmer for 2 more minutes.

9. Serve once piping hot.

"Where you will be in ten years from now depends on what journey you decide to take today".

Giovanni L Malacrino

Six Cheese Pasta Explosion

Allergies
Gluten, Lactose

Intolerances
Dairy, Wine

You will need

- 300g Fusilli pasta
- Olive oil
- 50g salted butter
- 100g mushrooms, sliced
- ½ an onion, sliced
- 2 garlic cloves, finely chopped
- ½ red chilli, finely chopped
- Salt
- Pepper
- 25ml Vodka
- 50g mozzarella
- 50g Morbier au lait cru
- 50g Gorgonzola
- 50g Jarlsberg
- 50g Applewood cheese
- 100g peas
- 25g curry powder
- 50ml red wine
- 200ml cream
- 150g parmesan

Equipment

- Saucepan
- Sauté pan

Cooking method

1. Begin cooking the fusilli pasta in boiling water.
2. While the pasta is cooking, add the olive oil and butter to a sauté pan.
3. Once the butter is melted, add the mushrooms, onion, garlic cloves, ½ red chilli, and salt and pepper.
4. Leave to cook for a few minutes, before adding a splash of vodka.
5. Once the vegetables are soft, add the mozzarella, Morbier au lait cru, Gorgonzola, Jarlsberg and Applewood cheeses to the pan.
6. As the cheese begins to melt, check on your pasta. Once it is soft, drain it and add to sauté pan. Shake to spread the ingredients evenly.
7. Keep mixing the cheese into the pasta continuously until fully melted.
8. Add the curry powder, red wine, cream and parmesan cheese. Continue to mix together until the parmesan has melted.
9. Once piping hot, serve.

"When making a decision,
keep your emotions out of it".

Helen Schucman

Seared Scallops and Baby Octopus served with Samphire

Allergies
Crustaceans, Molluscs, Lactose

Intolerances
Dairy, Wine

You will need
- 200g scallops
- 150g baby octopus
- White wine
- 1 tbsp butter
- 25ml Pernod
- 1 tbsp olive oil
- 1 tbsp finely chopped basil
- 1 tsp crushed garlic
- Salt and pepper to taste
- ¼ red chilli, deseeded and finely chopped

Equipment
- Griddle pan
- Wooden spoon
- Table spoon
- Tea spoon
- Saucepan

Cooking method

1. Add olive oil and butter to the griddle pan and heat on a high temperature, making sure the butter does not burn.

2. Once the butter has melted and is steaming hot, add the scallops with a dash of salt and pepper. Turn the heat down slightly and leave to cook for a minute.

3. Sprinkle over the finely chopped basil and chilli peppers, and leave to cook for a further two minutes.

4. While they're cooking, add the samphire to boiling water and leave to boil for three to four minutes. Flip the scallops over and add the calamari. Leave to cook for a further two minutes.

5. Once the samphire is cooked, drain and serve with a slab of butter.

6. Add a splash of white wine to the scallops, followed by a splash of Pernod and leave to cook for another minute.

7. Once the scallops are a golden colour, use a spoon to serve the seafood onto a plate.

8. Enjoy!

"Take control of your own life, embrace positivity and ignore negativity".

Giovanni L Malacrino

Seafood on a bed of Laverbread

Allergies
Shellfish, Lactose

Intolerances
Dairy, Eggs

You will need
For Laverbread Omelette
- 80g butter
- 3 cloves garlic
- 1 red chilli
- 1 bunch of Basil
- 450g laverbread
- 4 eggs
- 100g breadcrumbs
- 75g parmesan cheese
- Olive oil
- Salt and pepper
- White wine

You will need
For Seafood
- 3 cloves garlic
- 1 red chilli
- 1 bunch of basil
- 4 scallops
- 4 shrimps
- 8 cockles
- 6 mussels
- Olive oil
- Salt and pepper
- White wine

Equipment
- Frying pan
- Wooden spoon

Cooking method

1. Melt the butter in the sauté pan with a splash of olive oil.
2. Add the sliced garlic.
3. Gently pan fry.
4. Add the sliced chilli and basil and season with salt and pepper.
5. Add the laverbread.
6. Add the eggs and parmesan cheese.
7. Mix together.
8. Gently cook for a couple of minutes.
9. Flip.
10. Cook for a further two minutes.

In another sauté pan

11. Heat the olive oil.
12. Add the sliced garlic followed by basil and chilli.
13. Add in the following order, scallops, prawns, clams, mussels.
14. Season with salt and pepper.
15. Finish with a splash of white wine and cook for two minutes.
16. Ready to serve.
17. Place the laverbread on the plate and top with seafood.
18. Decorate with a couple of basil leaves.

"Confront your real issues and commit to change".

Stephen Truelove

Seafood Medley

Allergies
Shellfish, Lactose

Intolerances
Dairy

You will need
- Olive oil
- Salt
- Pepper
- 80g of butter
- 2 cloves of sliced garlic
- ½ chopped onion
- ½ chopped red onion
- 1 red chilli
- 1 bunch of basil
- 3 whole squids
  (head included)
- 10 clams
- 10 mussels
- 6 razor clams
- White wine
- 1 lemon
- 100 ml of fresh cream

Equipment
- Griddle pan
- Serving spoon
- Sharp knife

Cooking method

1. Melt the butter in the griddle pan with a splash of olive oil.
2. Add the sliced two half onions.
3. Gently pan fry.
4. Add the sliced, garlic, chilli and basil to the squids
5. Season with salt and pepper.
6. Gently pan fry for a couple of minutes.
7. Move the squids to one side of the griddle pan.
8. Add in the order clams, mussels and razor clams.
9. Season with salt and pepper.
10. Add a splash of white wine and the juice of half lemon.
11. Add the basil.
12. Finish with the fresh cream.
13. Cook for a further two minutes.
14. Ready to serve.

"When that mountain looks too high, just take one step at a time".

Stephen Truelove

You will need

- 10 large shrimps
- 1 salmon fillet
- 1 carrot
- 1 courgette
- ¼ broccoli
- 1 cup flour
- Cold water
- 200g parmesan cheese
- 1 bunch of basil
- 90g rocket salad
- 5 cherry tomatoes
- ½ red pepper
- Salt and pepper
- Olive oil

Equipment

- Frying pan
- Deep frying pan
- Serving spoon
- Sharp knife
- Pestle and mortar

Cooking method
For the batter
1. In a bowl mix flour and water.

2. Add salt and pepper.

3. Keep stirring till all mixed together.

For the pesto
1. Chop the basil leaves.

2. Mix the basil with olive oil in a bowl.

3. Add salt and pepper.

4. Keep bashing till smooth.

For the parmesan case
1. Heat the frying pan.

2. Pour the parmesan on the hot pan.

3. Cook for a couple of minutes.

4. Remove the parmesan.

5. Place on top of a bowl to shape it.

For the salmon
1. Remove the skin and cut into chunks.

For the vegetables
1. Cut the vegetables into chunks, roughly the same size of the salmon.

For the tempura
1. Heat the olive oil.

2. Deep the vegetables and the fish in the batter.

3. Fry one by one till gold.

Serve
- Place the parmesan case on a large plate.
- Fill the case with the vegetables, prawns and salmon.
- Decorate with the rocket salad, cherry tomatoes and red pepper.
- Sprinkle pesto over the top of the tempura.

Allergies
Lactose, Shellfish

Intolerances
Dairy

You will need
- 50g butter
- 1 tbsp olive oil
- 1 tbsp garlic, peeled and crushed
- 1 yellow pepper, sliced and deseeded
- 1 green pepper, sliced and deseeded
- 1 red pepper, sliced and deseeded
- 300g salmon
- 300g calamari rings
- 300g shrimps
- 250g mussels
- 1 tomato, diced into cubes
- 100g beetroot
- Salt
- Pepper
- Dried chilli
- 25ml Vodka
- 1 tbsp basil
- 1 tbsp squid ink
- 250g arborio rice
- 100g parmesan cheese
- 50ml coconut milk

Equipment
- Sauté pan
- Wooden spoon
- Sharp knife

Cooking method

1. Melt the butter the sauté pan with a splash of olive oil.
2. Once melted, add the garlic and chopped peppers and leave to fry for a minute.
3. Next, add the salmon, calamari rings and shrimp, stirring in between each ingredient.
4. Add the diced tomato and chopped beetroot and continue to cook for a further minute.
5. Season with salt, pepper and dried chilli.
6. Add another splash of olive oil and vodka.
7. Stir in the mussels to the pan and leave to cook on a high heat.
8. If there is not enough liquid, pour in some water and leave to boil.
9. Sprinkle over some chopped basil leaves.
10. Spoon in the squid ink and evenly stir into the pan.
11. Once the squid ink has covered all the ingredients, pour in the arborio rice and stir so it is evenly covering the pan.
12. Add some vegetable stock to help the risotto boil and release its flavours.
13. Stir continuously so that the risotto does not stick to the pan.
14. Leave to simmer for a few minutes, before adding the parmesan cheese.
15. Just before serving, add the coconut milk.
16. Once the risotto is a thick, creamy texture, it can be served.

Did you know...

Adding a splash of vodka to a dish, whilst it's cooking, brings out flavours from ingredients such as tomatoes, which can't be released with just water or fat. **Just watch out for the flame!**

Peppered Steak with Creamy Mushroom Sauce

Allergies
Lactose, Mustard

Intolerances
Dairy

You will need
- 1 fresh red pepper
- 200g mushrooms, sliced
- 2 garlic cloves, peeled and finely chopped
- Fresh basil and parsley
- 2 steaks
- 50g butter
- 25g mascarpone
- 25ml vodka
- 100 ml red wine
- 3 tsp mustard
- 1 onion, peeled and chopped
- Extra virgin olive oil
- 300ml cream
- 200g Italian sausage, sliced

Equipment
- Frying pan
- Griddle pan

Cooking method

1. Heat olive oil in the frying pan over a medium to high heat until it begins to bubble.

2. Add the chopped garlic, mushrooms and pepper. Leave to fry in the oil, shaking the pan to spread the ingredients around.

3. Add the sliced Italian sausage and continue to fry on a high heat.

4. Season with salt and pepper to taste.

5. Add a slab of butter and the chopped onions into the pan and stir into the other ingredients.

6. Add the parsley leaves. Continue to shake.

7. Pour in the red wine. Bring to the boil and leave to simmer for 3 minutes.

8. Add a splash of vodka (Be careful of the flame!).

9. Stir the cream and mustard into the sauce.

10. Add the mascarpone cheese and leave to simmer on a low heat while you cook the steak(s).

11. Heat oil in a griddle pan over a medium to high heat, moving the pan around to ensure the oil covers the base.

12. Once the oil is hot, place your steak(s) onto the pan and season with salt and pepper.

13. Add a splash of brandy (Another flame!).

14. Cook the steaks to your liking and place on a plate.

15. Pour over the sauce and garnish with parsley leaves.

16. Serve.

Chicken and Vegetable Stir Fry

Cooking tip
Woks are thinner than regular frying pans. This means they heat up quicker, so it is really important to keep moving your food around to avoid it from burning!

Allergies
Soy

Intolerances
N/A

You will need

- 4 diced chicken breasts
- ½ red chilli, sliced (optional)
- A pinch of ginger
- 500g mixed vegetables such as broccoli, kale and carrots
- 1½ tbsp tamari
- Soy sauce
- 2 tbsp Tamarind paste
- 1 tsp Chinese five spice
- Stock
- Olive oil
- Salt and pepper to taste

Equipment

- Griddle pan
- Frying pan
- Wooden spoon

Cooking method

1. Heat the oil in a large griddle pan, then fry the chilli, ginger and chicken.

2. Once the chicken is cooked, transfer the contents of the griddle pan into a separate wok and leave on a low heat.

3. Pour the soy and chilli sauce into the now empty griddle pan, along with the Tamarind paste, Chinese five spice powder and a few splashes of olive oil. Leave to simmer over a high heat.

4. Once the liquid is bubbling steadily, add the vegetables. Spread them evenly across the pan, allowing them to cook throughout.

5. Leave to cook for a further 5 minutes.

6. Once the vegetables are cooked, add them to the chicken and fry altogether for 1 minute.

7. While that's cooking, repeat step 2 to create the sauce again. Once this is bubbling, pour it in with the chicken and vegetables.

8. Season with salt and pepper.

9. Serve.

"You can grow from an experience, or you can create blame from it".

Stephen Truelove

You will need

- Olive oil
- 50g garlic crushed
- 8oz Rib-eye steak, cut into strips
- 300g chicken, cut into strips
- 300g lamb, cut into strips
- 100ml water
- 100g basil leaves
- 500g mixed peppers
- 100g spring onion, diced
- 300g mushrooms
- 200g broccoli
- 200g cauliflower
- 250g purple kale
- Salt and pepper
- 50g diced tomatoes

Equipment

- Griddle pan
- Wok
- Large wooden/metal spoon

Cooking method

1. Add a splash of oil to the griddle pan and sauté half of your garlic.

2. Once the garlic is simmering, add your steak strips.

3. Next, add your chicken strips. Make sure your meat is spread out across the pan, so it all cooks evenly.

4. Leave the meat to cook, shaking occasionally for a few minutes before adding the lamb.

5. After 5 minutes, pour in the water. This will create a flavoursome stock for later.

6. Sprinkle over the basil leaves. Give it a thorough stir and leave on a medium heat for 5 minutes or until the meat is cooked all the way through.

7. Once the meat is cooked, take the griddle pan off the heat and put to one side.

8. Place your wok on a high heat and add a splash of olive oil. Sauté the other half of your garlic.

9. Once simmering, add the mixed peppers and leave to cook for a few minutes or until the peppers begin to singe.

10. Chuck in the diced spring onions, mushrooms, cauliflower and broccoli. Shake the pan so the vegetables are evenly spread. Leave to cook for 5 minutes, stirring occasionally.

11. Next, add the purple kale and continue cooking on a high heat for 5 minutes.

12. When the vegetables are soft, add the cooked meat to the wok, including the juices from the griddle pan.

13. Season with salt and pepper.

14. Add the tomatoes and asparagus.

15. Stir all together and leave to cook on a medium heat for a further 2 minutes.

16. Take off the heat and serve.

Surf 'n' Turf Steak with Shrimp

Allergies
Fish, Molluscs, Lactose, Shellfish

Intolerances
Dairy

You will need

- 20ml olive oil
- 4 garlic cloves, finely cut
- ½ onion, finely cut
- 1 mushroom, finely cut
- ½ red pepper, chopped into slices
- ½ red chilli
- 200g shrimp
- 50ml red wine
- 2 16oz fillet steaks
- Salt
- Pepper
- Dried chilli
- 25g butter

Equipment

- Griddle pan
- Sauté pan

Cooking method

1. Add oil to sauté pan and heat up. Once hot, add the garlic, onion and mushrooms. Leave to cook for 2 minutes.

2. Once the vegetables begin to soften, add the cut up red pepper and chilli. Leave to cook on a high heat for a further 3 minutes.

3. Add the shrimps to the pan, followed by a splash of red wine. Leave to cook on a low to medium heat for 3 minutes.

4. In the griddle pan, add a splash of olive oil and the butter and put on a high heat. Once the butter has melted, add the steaks.

5. Season the steaks with salt and pepper. Once cooked to your liking, transfer onto a plate.

6. Once the shrimps are cooked, serve them and the vegetables with the steak. Make sure you serve with all the juices too!

"Your mind has the map to your freedom".

Stephen Truelove

Your notes

Here are some quick healthy alternatives that you can drink on the go!!

You will need

- 1 small bunch of kale
- 4 celery stalks
- Half a cucumber

Equipment

- Sharp knife
- Chopping board
- Blender

Did you know?

Regularly drinking green smoothies can dramatically improve your health.
The delicious drinks can actually help with natural weight loss, boosting your energy throughout the day, strengthening your immune system and so much more.

Kale is great for aiding healthy digestion due to its high fibre content.

Celery is jam-packed full of good stuff, from antioxidants to Vitamin K to help your body respond to injuries.

Cucumbers help you stay hydrated and nourished with a whole host of vitamins.

Allergies
Celery

Intolerances
N/A

Cooking method

1. Cut the bunch of kale into small, fine pieces.
2. Cut the cucumber into small dices.
3. Cut the celery stalks into small chunks.
4. Place ingredients into a blender and blend for two minutes, or until completely liquefied.

"One thing for sure is that the last minute has now gone and is now just a memory".

Giovanni L Malacrino

Power Breakfast Smoothie

Allergies
N/A

Intolerances
N/A

You will need
- One apple
- 3 small carrots
- Half a cucumber

Equipment
- Knife
- Peeler
- Chopping board
- Blender

Cooking method

1. Slice the apple into segments.
2. Remove the pips, core and stem.
3. Peel the carrots and chop into small chunks.
4. Cut the cucumber into small pieces.
5. Add ingredients into the blender and blend for two minutes or until completely liquefied.

Remember...

An apple a day keeps the doctor away! – And they're yummy.

"If you think you can't or you think you can, you're probably right".

Henry Ford

Did you know?
Almond milk is a great option for vegans and those who are intolerant or allergic to dairy milk.

Allergies
Nuts

Intolerances
N/A

You will need
- 150g raw almonds
- 2 cups of water and a bowl for soaking
- (Optional) Sweeteners e.g. sugar, honey or agave syrup for taste

Equipment
- Bowl
- Cup
- Blender
- Nut bag or cheesecloth

Cooking method

1. Soak the almonds overnight (Or longer! The longer the better) in a bowl of water.

2. Drain and rinse under cool running water.

3. Put almonds and water in a blender. Break up the almonds by pulsing the blender a couple of times.

4. Once broken up, blend continuously for a couple of minutes.

5. Strain the mixture through an opened nut bag or cheesecloth into a cup.

6. Gather the nut bag or cheesecloth around the mixture. Squeeze together to get out as much almond milk as possible into the cup.

7. If you like it a bit sweeter, add sugar, honey, agave syrup or a different sweetener to get it just right.

"It's not what you want that matters, it's why you want it".

Giovanni L Malacrino

"*Positive thoughts,
better outcomes*"!

Stephen Truelove

Various studies suggest children who take part in regular family meals are less likely to be overweight or delinquent, more likely to eat more healthier foods, have greater academic achievement, improved psychological well-being and more positive family interactions. These findings are based on studies below.

Who wouldn't want their children to have these positive effects just through eating good hearty meals together?

Extracts taken from Cornell University College of Human Ecology. Department of policy analysis and management.

Do family meals really make a difference?
By: Eliza Cook and Rachel Dunifon.
www.human.cornell.edu/sites/default/files/PAM/Parenting/Family-Mealtimes-2.pdf

Ref: Kelly Musick & Ann Meier Family dinners and adolescent well being.

Ref: (Fulkerson, Kubik & Fiese, 2011. Neumark-Sztainer, Hannan, Story, Croll & Perry 2003)

Shopping supply ideas for an emergency unexpected guest visit

- Oats
- Raisins
- Digestive biscuits
- Arborio rice (white rice stores better than brown rice)
- Selection of dry pastas
- Frozen ravioli pasta
- Tinned plum tomatoes
- Fresh eggs
- Selection of cheeses
- Parmesan cheese (can be frozen in small sachets)
- Sliced bacon
- Cured meats vacuum packed that can also be frozen
- Prawns
- Mussels
- Peanut butter
- Selection of beans in tins or packets
- Mixed pulses (lentils, mixed bean, black beans, etc.)
- Canned fruits and vegetables
- Frozen and canned meats (including ham, tuna, corned beef and chicken)
- Milk, fresh and long life
- Butter
- Bread
- Long life cream
- Dried mushrooms
- Wine for cooking and drinking
- Water and soft drinks
- Fresh and dried coconut
- Coconut oil
- Fresh garlic
- Basil from a plant and freeze leaves
- Plain and self-raising flour
- Yeast
- Nuts
- Olive oil
- Vinegar
- Honey
- Sugar
- Jams
- Salt and pepper
- A selection of vegetable, meat and fish stock

Some of the foods you can freeze.
Add your favourites to this list.

Foods you shouldn't freeze:
Milk – it becomes lumpy once thawed (but this can be OK for cooking)
Deep-fried food – after defrosting, the crispy coating will turn to mush
Sour cream – it can be alright for cooking but will separate after freezing
Dishes with crumb toppings – it will lose the crispness and go soggy.

Freezing tips:
- Let all fresh food reach room temperature before freezing.
- Make the most of your ice cube tray – Giovanni suggests blending herbs with water or olive oil and freezing in a tray. Wine can also be frozen as ice cubes which you can use to keep your drink cool without diluting it or pop it into your cooking, and stock can also be frozen in a tray, which will save you time.
- Make sure all produce is frozen in a sealed container.
- Meat in particular needs to be properly wrapped.
- Be aware that anything that has a high water content, like lettuce, will not taste as good after being frozen and then defrosted.
- Freeze everything when it's fresh.
- Defrost all meats thoroughly before cooking,
- Items such as bread for toasting can be cooked straight from the freezer.
- **Remember**: never refreeze raw meat that has been frozen and then thawed – you can, however, freeze cooked meat that was frozen when raw.
- Always make sure the freezer is defrosted and isn't packed so full that air can't circulate.

Your notes

Getting into the buying zone is the most important part of any form of cooking; you can cook from a recipe book or make up your own recipes, but you might ask yourself 'how do I know what to buy?' You've got to understand textures, smells and tastes of different ingredients.

What I would suggest is visiting your local supermarket, delicatessen, international food shop or anywhere that sells herbs and spices. When you have chosen an item, simply pick them up, feel them and smell them.

You can smell a chilli pepper and tell if it's hot or not. Regardless of experience you must start somewhere the same as everything in life, whether it's rock climbing, playing football or mountain climbing, you get better with time and cooking is the same. When you start cooking, you must learn about the dishes you're going to be cooking and what you're doing is getting your senses used to smelling certain items and if you believe in your subconscious then it'll help you to decide what to put in which dish. Go into a variety of shops and just learn how things smell and feel...people may look at you funny in the supermarket because you're picking up peppers and really smelling them, but you need to train and practice.

When you get home, slice the vegetables up and smell them again; it will really help you know what goes together well as certain ingredients won't mix together well, you can either follow a recipe or have even more fun making up your own recipes, and this book is all about having fun.

That's how you get into the buying zone.

Share your knowledge, don't share your book. You may never get it back!

Stephen Truelove

Feed your mind
Feed your soul
And life will be wonderful

Giovanni L Malacrino

Answer: I choose pasta because I choose pasta. Because you just choose it, there is no justification. You just choose it.
Try this out next time someone asks you to make a decision between one thing and another. **Just choose!**

Awaken The Giant Within
Anthony Robbins
ISBN 13: 978-0671791544

Who Moved My Cheese?
Dr Spencer Johnson
ISBN 13: 978-0091816971

FISH!
Stephen C. Lundin, Harry Paul,
John Christensen
ISBN: 978-1444792805

1 Minute Management Meets the Monkey
Kenneth Blanchard and William Oncken Jr.
ISBN: 978-0007116980

NLP Workbook
Joseph O'Connor
ISBN 13: 978-0007100033

Change Your Life in 7 Days
Paul McKenna
ISBN 13: 978-0593066614

Gino's Hidden Italy
Gino DeACampo
ISBN: 978-147364690

Ultimate Fit Food
Gordon Ramsay
ISBN: 978-1473652286

The Power of Now
Eckhart Tolle
ISBN: 978-0340733509

A Journey of Discovery and Self-learning
Stephen Truelove
ISBN: 9781095617571

You Can Heal Your Life
Louise L. Hay
ISBN-13: 978-093761101

Men Are From Mars, Women Are From Venus
John Gray
ISBN: 978-0007152599

Get The Life You Want
Dr Richard Bandler
ISBN 13: 978-000729516

Ask And It Is Given
Esther Hicks
ISBN: 1401904599

The Celestine Prophecy
James Redfield
ISBN: 978-0553409024

Rich Dad Poor Dad
Robert T. Kiyosaki,
Sharon Lechter
ISBN: 978-1612680194

Franco and Friends: food from the Walnut Tree
Ann & Franco Taruschio
ISBN: 978-0563383765

The Secret
Rhonda Byrne
ISBN 13: 978-1471172397

**Left Brain Right Brain
Whole Brain Thinking**
Martyn Ward
ASIN: B00E66Q6CA

Master Networking
Tracey Smolinski
ISBN: 978-1786153289

Three Feet from Gold
Sharon L. Lechter
ISBN: 978-1402784798

**Lord Sugar:
The Man Who Revolutionised
British Business**
Charlie Burden
ISBN 13: 978-1844549290

**The 10X Rule:
The Only Difference Between
Success and Failure**
Grant Cardone
ISBN: 978-0470627600

*You already have
all the resources you require
to succeed at what you want,
you just haven't realized it yet!!*

Stephen Truelove

"Ask yourself,
Am I happy on the inside?
If not, do something about it".

Giovanni L Malacrino